Dragons for Resilience
A Coloring Meditation Journal

By
Oju Ayọ

Volume III

Dragons for Resilience
A Coloring Meditation Journal

By
Oju Ayọ

Volume III

For my nieces & nephews
thank you for shining so brilliantly
I love you

published by Oju Ayo LLC, Brooklyn, NY, Albany, NY
email any inquiries to oju.ayo.golden@gmail.com

visit me on the web! ojuayo.com

the illustrations in this book were rendered in Sakura Pigma Micron pens.
book designed by Oju Ayọ

library of congress catalog card number;
pending

first printing

ISBN 978-1-7348297-2-3

When I was five years old, I moved in with my grandparents. I loved it. Their house looked like Hansel and Gretel would come visiting at any moment.

While I lived with them, I started kindergarten which was only a ten minute walk up the street. Somehow my teacher found out that my dad was from Africa (I probably told her). She asked me if I knew African dance, "Sure," I said, not giving it a second thought.

Later that week, on my way back from lunch-time recess, I saw long lines of children headed toward my classroom. I wondered what cool activity was waiting for them there. Upon my own arrival to my classroom, I noticed the accordion wall that separated our room from the next had been neatly folded back. I also noticed our desks and portable cubbies had all been moved out of the way.

At the front, near the blackboard, was a rolling cart with a record player on it. Propped against the record player was an album cover. Before I recognized the dancing figures, the teacher gleefully pointed to me and announced: "Today, this young lady will teach us African dance!"

I must have been riding on playground adrenaline, because I hopped up there without hesitation. I could barely see the endless rows of crowded children waiting for my choreography. The teacher placed the needle on the vinyl.

I shouted the command, "Go like this!" then "Go like that!"

We jumped, we shimmied, we spun around. To me, it was a glorious game of "Simon Says." Of course, when requested, I could never do the same move twice. I simply suggested I had another move I was sure they would love and continued to let whatever came to me spill from my feet.

When I got home, my grandmother told me that my teacher called. My heart screeched to a stop. I knew my grandmother knew that I didn't know anything about African dance. What did my teacher say? Was I in trouble?

"Your teacher thanked me, she said you were a delight," my grandmother said.

That was that. We never talked about it again.

I used to remember this story with a tinge of guilt, a delayed ear-warming embarrassment. But when recently recounting this tale to a friend, I realized that I took what could have been a humiliating situation and gave it a shot of kindergarten-style magic. To this day, I use tools formed in me way back then. It is still important to me to cultivate the habit of showing up and digging deep into my creativity to give my best effort.

The dragon drawings in this meditation journal were born at a time when I thought my circumstances would not only humiliate me but crush me to dust. Instead of dust, I found resilience.

I invite you to seek out a quiet place, maybe play some music, and let the wisdom of the accompanying quotes wash over you while you use coloring to reflect on the ways you can keep showing up for yourself.

Adapt what is useful,
reject what is useless,
and add what is
specifically
your own.

Bruce Lee

Bruce Lee (1940 – 1973)
was an actor, film director, martial artist, martial
arts instructor, philosopher, and founder of the
martial art Jeet Kune Do, one of the wushu or
kung fu styles. He is widely considered to be
one of the most influential martial artists of all
time, and a pop culture icon of the 20th century.
He is often credited with helping to change
the way Asian people were presented in
American films.

What keeps me going
is that quest
for just being able
to be present and be myself.
Not for people, but for me.

Janet Mock

Janet Mock (born on March 10, 1983)
is an author, TV host, and transgender rights
activist. Her debut book, the memoir *Redefining
Realness*, became a New York Times bestseller.
She is a contributing editor for *Marie Claire*.

I think one of the things
I'm most proud of in myself
is that I'm okay to fail
in front of the world;
I'm okay to make mistakes
and get back up
and try again.

Solange Knowles

Solange Knowles (born on June 24, 1986),
is a singer, songwriter, model, and actress.
Her third studio album, *A Seat at the Table* (2016)
became her first number-one album in the United
States. The album's first single, "Cranes in the Sky"
won the Grammy for Best R&B Performance.
Billboard magazine ranked her as the 100th most
successful dance artist of all-time. In 2017 Solange
was honored with the "Impact Award" at Billboard
Women in Music.

I was not going to let
people tell me
what I'm capable of.

Colin Kaepernick

Colin Kaepernick (born on November 3, 1987)
is a football quarterback who is currently a free
agent. In 2016, Kaepernick became a national
figure when he stirred vehement controversy by
kneeling while the United States national anthem
was being played at the start of NFL games.
The choice to kneel was to call attention to the
issues of racial inequality and police brutality in the
U.S. while also attempting to honor the members
of the U.S. military. Kaepernick also pledged to
donate one million dollars to "organizations working
in oppressed communities." Amnesty International
honored Kaepernick with the 2018 Ambassador
of Conscience Award.

**Now I choose
to make a personal decision
and to empower myself
to regain my life...
It's important for me
to now move on.**

Ron Dellums

Ronald Dellums (1935 - 2018)
was a politician who served as Oakland's forty-eighth
(and third Black) mayor. From 1971 to 1998, he was
elected to thirteen terms as a Member of the U.S.
House of Representatives from Northern California's
9th Congressional District, after which he worked as
a lobbyist in Washington D.C. Dellums was the first
Black congressmen elected to Congress from Northern California and the first openly socialist successful
non-incumbent Congressional candidate since World
War II. When President Ronald Reagan vetoed
Dellums' Comprehensive Anti-Apartheid Act of 1986,
a Democratic-controlled House and a Republi-
can-controlled Senate overrode Reagan's veto,
the first override of a presidential foreign policy veto
in the 20th century.

Start where you are.
Use what you have.
Do what you can.

Arthur Ashe

Arthur Ashe (1943 – 1993)
was a professional tennis player who won
three Grand Slam titles. Ashe was the first
Black player selected to the United States
Davis Cup team and the only black man
ever to win the singles title at Wimbledon,
the US Open, and the Australian Open.
He was ranked World No. 1 by Harry
Hopman in 1968 and by Lance Tingay
of The Daily Telegraph and World Tennis
Magazine in 1975. In the ATP computer
rankings, he peaked at No. 2 in May 1976.
He retired in 1980. He founded the Arthur
Ashe Foundation for the Defeat of AIDS
and the Arthur Ashe Institute for Urban
Health. On June 20, 1993, Ashe was
posthumously awarded the Presidential
Medal of Freedom.

These who say
it can't be done
are usually interrupted
by others doing it.

James A. Baldwin

James Arthur Baldwin (1924 – 1987)
was a novelist and social critic. His essays,
as collected in *Notes of a Native Son* (1955),
explore intricacies of racial, sexual,
and class distinctions in Western societies,
most notably in mid-20th-century America.
Some of Baldwin's essays are book-length,
including *The Fire Next Time* (1963),
No Name in the Street (1972), and *The Devil
Finds Work* (1976). An unfinished manuscript,
Remember This House, was expanded
and adapted for cinema as the Academy
Award-nominated documentary film *I Am Not
Your Negro* that delves into black history
and ties the past Civil Rights Movement
to the present Black Lives Matter Movement.

They say
the two most important days
in a person's life
were the day you were born
and the day you discover
why you were born.

Viola Davis

Viola Davis (born on August 11, 1965)
is an actress, producer, feminist and an outspoken
supporter of the Civil Rights Movement. She was
the first Black actress to be nominated for three
Academy Awards, winning one, and is the only
Black person to date to win the Triple Crown
of Acting; an Oscar, an Emmy, and a Tony
in an acting category.

It is at this moment,
when things appear so bleak
that we must redouble our efforts
and not give up. We must believe
that we can remake the world
in a more peaceful reality.

Cynthia McKinney

Cynthia McKinney (born on March 17, 1955) is a politician and activist. As a member of the Democratic Party, she served six terms in the United States House of Representatives. She was the first Black woman elected to represent Georgia in the House. She left the Democratic Party and in 2008, ran as the Presidential candidate of the Green Party of the United States. In February 2010, McKinney was awarded the 'Peace through Conscience' award from the Munich American Peace Committee. McKinney has been featured in a full-length documentary titled *American Blackout*.

**Small acts,
when multiplied
by millions of people,
can transform
the world.**

Howard Zinn

Howard Zinn (1922 – 2010) was a historian, playwright, and social activist. He wrote extensively about the Civil Rights Movement and the Anti-war Movement, and labor history of the U.S. He was chair of the history and social sciences department at Spelman College, and a political science professor at Boston University. Zinn wrote more than twenty books, including his best-selling and influential *A People's History of the United States*. In 2007, he published a version of it for younger readers.

We don't create a fantasy
world to escape reality.
We create it
to be able to stay.

Lynda Barry

Lynda Barry (born on January 2, 1956)
is a cartoonist, author, and teacher.
Barry is best known for her weekly comic strip
Ernie Pook's Comeek. She garnered attention
with her 1988 illustrated novel
The Good Times are Killing Me, about
an interracial friendship between two young
girls, which was adapted into a play.
What It Is (2008) is a graphic novel that is part
memoir, part collage and part workbook,
in which Barry instructs her readers in
methods to open up their own creativity;
it won the comics industry's 2009 Eisner
Award for Best Reality-Based Work.

**If we give our children
sound self-love,
they will be able
to deal with whatever
life puts before them.**

bell hooks

bell hooks (born on September 25, 1952),
is an author, feminist, and social activist.
The focus of hooks' writing has been the
intersectionality of race, capitalism,
and gender, and what she describes as their
ability to produce and perpetuate systems
of oppression and class domination.
She has published over 30 books and
numerous scholarly articles, appeared
in documentary films, and participated in
public lectures. She has addressed race,
class, and gender in education, art, history,
sexuality, mass media, and feminism.
In 2014, she founded the bell hooks Institute
at Berea College in Berea, Kentucky.

The blues have hope wrapped inside them.

Andrea Davis Pinkney

Andrea Davis Pinkney
(born on September 25, 1963)
is a children's author and editor.
She is the author of more than 20 books and
was the founder of the "first African American
children's book imprint at a major publishing
company," Jump at the Sun at Hyperion Books
for Children, Disney Publishing Worldwide.
Her books have been awarded multiple
Coretta Scott King Book Awards
and Jane Addams Children's Literature
Honor citations, to name a few. She is also
vice president and editor-at-large for Scholastic Trade Books.

**Autumn is
a second spring
when every leaf
is a flower**

Albert Camus

Albert Camus (1913 – 1960)
was a philosopher, author,
and journalist. His views contribut-
ed to the rise of the philosophy
known as absurdism. He wrote
in his essay "The Rebel,"
that his whole life was devoted
to opposing the philosophy
of nihilism while still delving
deeply into individual freedom.
He won the Nobel Prize
in Literature at the age of 43
in 1957, the second youngest
recipient in history.

There is an energy within...
pure strength...
the energy of the person
which is put in different forms,
in different shapes...
Once we discover that energy
I think that such a thing
as dance becomes such a delight
because you're moving on
a stream that is you
but it is even over and beyond you.

Katherine Dunham

Katherine Dunham (1909 – 2006)
was a dancer, choreographer, author, educator, and social activist.
Known for developing the Dunham Technique, Dunham had one of the most
successful dance careers in American and European theater for the 20th century, and directed her own dance company for 30 years. She has been called the
"matriarch and queen mother of Black dance." The Katherine Dunham Dance
Company was the only self-supported Black dance troupe in the U.S. during
the 1940's and 50's, and throughout her extensive career, she choreographed
more than ninety individual dances. Dunham was an innovator in modern
dance as well as a leader in the field of ethnochoreology.

CPSIA information can be obtained
at www.ICGtesting.com
Printed in the USA
BVHW090524310820
587640BV00001B/3